Tarantulas

Trace Taylor

This big spider is a tarantula.

Some tarantulas are as big as a plate.

legs

arms

arms

legs

Tarantulas have eight legs and two arms.

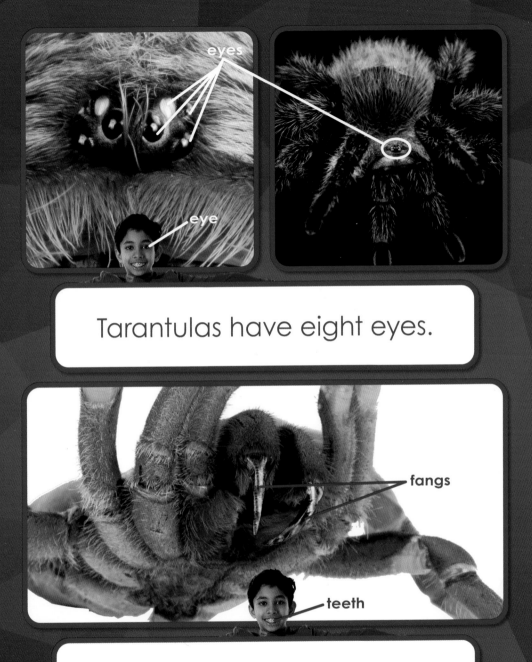

eyes

eye

Tarantulas have eight eyes.

fangs

teeth

They have two big fangs.

mouth

mouth

Tarantulas have a mouth.

hair

They have hair.

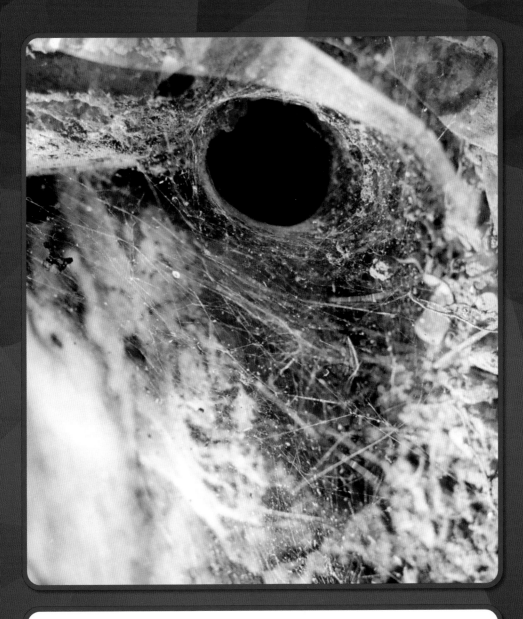

Many tarantulas live in holes.

The holes can be in the dirt.

The holes can be in trees.

Tarantulas put out
webs from the holes.

A bug is on the web.

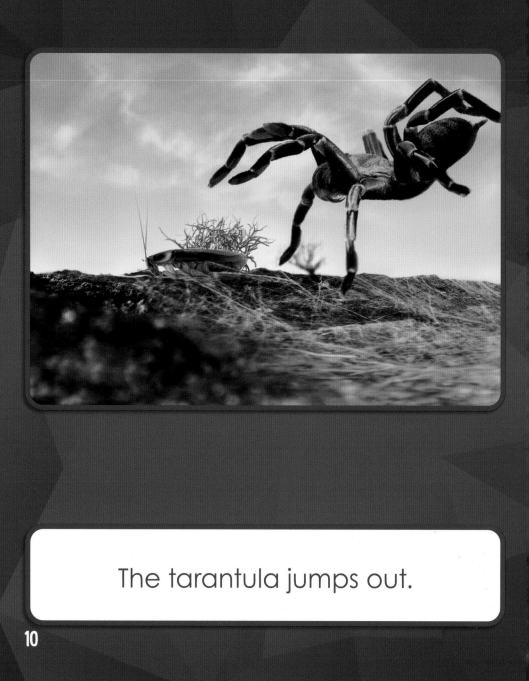

The tarantula jumps out.

It puts the fangs into the bug.

Now the tarantula can eat.

Tarantulas eat lots
of animals.

They love to eat bugs.

They can eat mice.

They can eat frogs.

They can eat lizards.

They can eat little birds.

But tarantulas have to look out.

All of these animals
can eat them, too!

Tarantula Body Parts

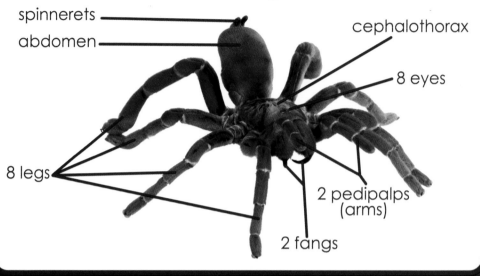

spinnerets

abdomen

cephalothorax

8 eyes

8 legs

2 pedipalps
(arms)

2 fangs

Goliath Birdeater

The largest tarantula on record lives in the rainforests of South America. It can be as big as a dinner plate, and its fangs can be an inch long. It's called the Goliath birdeater. This big spider can make hissing noises that sound very dangerous. Its bite, though very painful, isn't poisonous to people.

Tarantula Facts

There are more than 800 kinds of tarantulas in the world. Most are harmless to humans, but there are a few tarantulas in Asia, Africa, and Australia whose venom can cause serious reactions or illness. Very few people have ever died from a tarantula's bite. Some people like to keep the hairy arachnids as pets!

Cobalt Blue

King Baboon

Thai Zebra

Gooty Sapphire Ornamental

Power Words

How many can you read?

1G

	be	it	of
	big	little	on
a	can	live	the
all	have	look	they
and	in	lots	this
are	is	love	to

2G

	eat	many	them
	eight	now	these
animal	from	out	too
as	into	put	two
but	jump	some	